Date Due

The First North Americans

How Men Learned to Live in North America

Margaret K. Zieman

McClelland and Stewart Limited

illustrated by Merle Smith
designed by Brant Cowie

The illustration of the Mound Builders' community on pages 36-37 is based on an artist's conception which appeared in National Geographic, *December, 1972.*

ISBN 0-7710-9075-7

McClelland and Stewart Limited
The Canadian Publishers
25 Hollinger Road
Toronto, Ontario

Printed and bound in Canada.

CONTENTS

Man in North America: Map   *4*

Chapter I   The Ice Age Hunters   *5*

Chapter II   North America's First Cave Men   *10*

Chapter III   America's First Farmers   *14*

Chapter IV   Early Craftsmen: The Basket Makers   *20*

Chapter V   The Ghost Cities in the Cliffs   *25*

Chapter VI   The Shellfish Eaters   *30*

Chapter VII   The Mysterious Mound Builders   *34*

Chapter VIII   Baby Faces in the Jungle   *40*

Chapter IX   The Aztecs   *46*

Chapter X   Status Seekers of Canada's North-west Coast   *51*

Chapter XI   The Woodland People   *57*

Chapter XII   Then the White Men Came   *62*

Chapter XIII   Horsemen of the Great Plains   *69*

Chapter XIV   The End of the Trail   *73*

Chapter XV   Indians of Canada — East of the Great Lakes   *79*

Chapter XVI   Indians of Western Canada   *85*

Chapter XVII   The Eskimos — Men of the Arctic   *90*

Man in North America: Historical Table   *95*

Further Reading   *96*

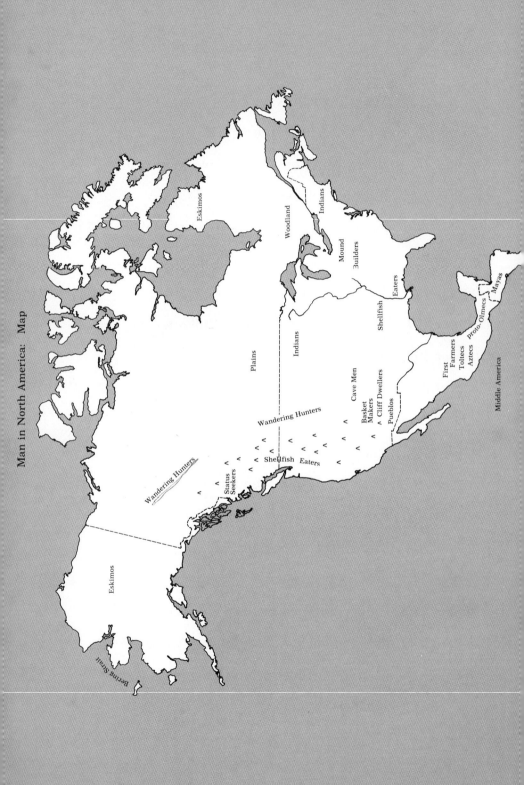

Man in North America: Map

Chapter I

THE
ICE
AGE
HUNTERS

Who discovered North America? Columbus? The Norsemen? Both answers are wrong. The first people to reach this western continent were prehistoric Ice Age hunters, who were the ancestors of America's present-day Indians and Eskimos. Because these men did not write about what they did, we cannot be sure of events which happened so long ago. But most scientists think that North America's first immigrants were a Stone Age people who came to this continent perhaps as long as 25,000 years ago. They came at a time when the vast glaciers of the last Ice Age were beginning to retreat and shrink. These folk crossed from Asia to North America by way of a land-bridge. At that time the bridge connected north-eastern Asia with America at the point where they still almost touch each other, in Alaska.

These journeys took place thousands of years before man learned to write and to keep the records which we call history; so this far-distant time is called the Prehistoric period. These newcomers are called Stone Age men because they lived at a time when men's tools and weapons were largely stone ones, although these people also used bone, wood, and antler.

Stone Age men knew nothing about using such metals as copper, bronze, or iron. They lived by hunting and fishing, and by gathering whichever wild plant foods they could find – roots, berries, herbs, and seeds of plants, which they had not yet learned to grow. Stone Age folk found shelter in caves, first driving out fierce wild bears and wolves.

We know about the Stone Age people because we can still see drawings on the walls of their cave homes in Spain and southern France. They show the animals they hunted for food – mammoth, bison, and reindeer. Here also were found stone tools and spear-points which they chipped from flint, the hardest of stones. Similar tools and weapons have been found on many prehistoric sites, not only in the Old World but also in North and South America.

Such objects are often the only records of man's existence in these prehistoric times. But the earth itself is a kind of book. By studying its various rock layers, called strata, experts can tell us about the different stages which North America passed through before it became what it is today. None of these earliest stages contain any evidence of man,

such as stone tools or weapons. Thus we know that mankind was not present on this continent earlier than 25,000 years ago. Before that time a series of Ice Ages, each lasting thousands of years, covered much of North America with vast ice sheets 9,000 feet thick. Because of this ice America must have been unpeopled until those first Stone Age men crossed from Asia to America thousands of years ago.

But why did they leave Asia and come to North America? First, they were wandering hunters. They had no permanent homes, for they followed the wild animals which supplied them with food and clothing. Without game, they couldn't stay alive. We cannot see them too clearly, these people who are almost hidden in the mists of prehistoric time. But we believe that they came to America to follow the game on which their lives depended. During the last Ice Age, which also covered both Europe and most of Asia, the wild creatures in Asia moved eastward and northward. They fled the increasing sleet, ice, and snow, which touched this north-eastern part of Asia very little. But the world got colder, the plant life got scarcer, and animal life moved north and eastward ahead of the moving ice. And the Stone Age hunters followed.

These people weren't trying to seek a new land. They were merely trying to stay alive, so they too drifted northward and eastward, following the game. They probably didn't even realize that they had crossed a land-bridge to a new continent. The bridge, we are told, may have been one hundred miles wide.

Nor did this prehistoric trek take place in one or two months – or even in one or two years. It continued for generations. Each generation found the increasing cold harder to bear. But still they moved on, following the game – with the ice closing in behind them.

They never travelled in large groups or even in tribes. The first Americans arrived in little straggly bands, probably family groups headed by the strongest man, with his wives, his sons and daughters with their families, and perhaps his brothers and their families. They came on foot, with only those tools and weapons which they could carry.

What did they look like, these first North Americans? They were definitely Asiatics, but they lacked many of the distinct features of modern Asiatic people, such as slanting eyes. They were probably shorter than today's Indians, but with similar straight, coarse black hair. Since these groups of wandering hunters did not arrive on this continent all at once, there were many distinctly different types. Prehistoric skulls found in America show that they had rather long heads with slanting foreheads, flat noses, broad cheek bones, and jaws which stuck out sharply in front.

You might not think too much of their looks, but they were nonetheless true men – *homo sapiens* (thinking man). Their ability to think ahead raised them above the level of animals. They had learned to make crude stone tools. It was not just luck which permitted man to survive the hardships of that final Ice Age. He was not only strong, but unlike wild creatures he could adapt more easily to changing conditions. That's why man has managed to survive through thousands of years, and to make progress, despite unfavourable living conditions.

These amazing people came a long way through ice and cold in quest of food and safety. They reached the end of their world and found another. They crouched around their campfires for protection against the bitter cold, wearing rough skins and eating fresh-killed game. Their weapons, probably some sort of throwing stick, along with chipped stone points for spear-heads, were always close at hand.

Actually these first North Americans did find a better land. Much of what is today Alaska, as well as the Mackenzie Valley, were ice-free. The valley offered these Ice Age hunters a passageway into the middle of our continent. How they moved ever southward, still following the game, until mankind had spread over two continents, will be told in the next chapter.

Chapter II

NORTH AMERICA'S FIRST CAVE MEN

Many Indian legends tell how man first came from the darkness deep within the earth, climbing upward to reach the sunlight. In these legends there is no hint of another continent from which their ancestors came. But we know that they moved from the snow and cold and winter darkness of Ice Age Asia into the easier, brighter life of this newly-discovered western world, where game was plentiful.

They came in many different groups and at many different times over thousands of years. Like the animals they hunted, men moved southward in North America over the centuries. As these earliest newcomers travelled southward, they kept well within the bounds of the ice-free corridor, hundreds of miles wide. It bordered the east side of the Rockies all the way from the Arctic. When those wandering hunters drifted for the first time into the great central plains of North America, they discovered a hunter's paradise. Game was everywhere. There they encountered the great prehistoric bison, with his horn-spread of six feet.

Groups of prehistoric hunters such as these might have stayed for one, two, or three generations in one area. But the urge to go on was strong, so they kept moving southward, always keeping the Rockies in sight. Perhaps the vast wide sea of long grass spreading eastward to an unknown horizon frightened these early North Americans. Few of them spread into the plains.

Many of them remained in the high plateau region of the American south-west, where today we find the most evidence of man's earliest presence in North America. Others moved on into the forests of Central and South America, following the rivers south and west into the mountain-hung valleys of the Andes. Then on they went through forest and plain until they finally stood at the southernmost tip of South America, looking far off into the Antarctic. They could go no farther, for they had reached the end of another continent.

But wherever they went they left their traces: chipped stone spear-points, stone grinding tools, the remains of cooking ashes, even a footprint beside the footprints of many animals which have long since died out. So far, few skeletons of these Ice Age hunters have been discovered. But the route they took as they moved southward is shown by a series of campsites. On these sites have been found their tools and weapons, as well as the bones of the mammoth, the elephant, the camel, and the giant ground sloth. There were also early forms of the bison and the horse, which was native to North America, but which finally migrated to Asia just before the last Ice Age ended. Many of these animals no longer live in America.

Such prehistoric campsites have been discovered as far north as Saskatchewan. Most of them have been found in the south-western United States, near the headwaters of the great streams which flow eastward from the Rockies. The sites follow a pattern along the route men travelled, always holding the mountains in sight and moving southward from stream to stream, where thickets of pine and cottonwood offered shelter.

It was near the headwaters of one such stream, the Cimarron in western New Mexico, near a cowtown called Folsom, that the most exciting discovery was made in 1926. Just by chance, a wandering cowboy happened to glance down the steep sides of a stream bank newly-cut by floods. He spotted some queer-looking bones sticking out many feet below. The bones were identified as those of an Ice Age bison. In the skeletal ribs was found a chipped stone spear-point of an unusual type. It was fluted, that is, grooved, on both sides near the base in order to fasten the point more securely to the shaft. It was called a Folsom point, after the area in which it was found.

Other Folsom points have been discovered both east of the Rockies and in the Great Basin, the high plateau region of the American south-west between the Rocky and Cascade Mountains. The men who made these special spear-points are known as Folsom men. They hunted the mammoth, the mastodon, the giant sloth, and the giant bison, which roamed North America 15,000 years ago.

Caves in the high plateau region of the south-western United States sheltered these Ice Age hunters from the high moisture and heavy rainfall of that period. In Canada and in north-eastern United States, this moisture froze into a great ice cap. But in this southern plateau region the moisture did not freeze, but formed great shallow lakes, which no longer exist. In this region, Sandia Cave near Albuquerque, New Mexico, showed that earlier men had preceded those who made the fluted Folsom points. Digging there below several earth layers many feet thick, experts found Folsom spear-points, as well as scrapers, shaft-smoothers, and rubbing stones. But further below these Folsom deposits they discovered a layer which held tools and spear-points of a different type, made perhaps 5,000 years earlier.

In still other caves and campsites along the shores of an Ice Age lake, stone implements which the people left behind suggest that some groups were not mainly hunters. Their mortars, pestles, and grindstones seem to have been designed for grinding wild plant foods, nuts, seeds, roots, bulbs, and berries.

Could it be that men were beginning to realize that plants were possibly a more dependable source of food than animals? Man did not become a farmer suddenly. But once he learned that he could grow plant food he no longer depended only on hunting for food. Perhaps some accidentally dropped wild seeds took root and grew, marking the start of man's first crop and a step upward in man's development. Men started to farm in two or three different places in America about the same time.

Chapter III

AMERICA'S
FIRST
FARMERS

There is a beautiful Indian legend about the youthful Hiawatha, who was fasting as part of his ritual of manhood. He met in the forest a handsome youth named Mondamin, who had flowing golden hair and wore vivid green and yellow garments. He challenged Hiawatha to one wrestling match, then to another and another. Before the third match he warned Hiawatha that this time Mondamin would be killed.

Hiawatha had learned to love the youth and was overcome with grief. But Mondamin told him not to mourn. He instructed Hiawatha to bury him, piling the earth into a mound above his body. From that mound a blessing would come to the Indians from the Great Spirit, or Manitou. From the mound where Mondamin was buried, the legend relates, the first stalk of maize, or Indian corn, grew. The golden corn silk was like Mondamin's hair, and the leaves were like his green and yellow garments.

In songs, dances, legends, and religious ceremonies, the Indians of North America have celebrated the story of maize, or Indian corn. It is still the New World's main food crop. Almost everyone knows that the Indians grew corn, squash, and beans, but how they developed these plants over hundreds of years is a thrilling story.

Certainly, prehistoric men did not transform themselves suddenly from hunters to farmers. In fact, many never made this change at all. Those who did probably remained in the same region for a very long time before they thought of planting any of the wild roots, seeds, and fruits which they collected for food. It took long years of experience to learn which plants were safe to eat. Many different peoples all over

North America changed their entire way of life through farming, especially through corn.

Corn was probably not the first plant these prehistoric Indians attempted to grow for a more reliable source of food. Possibly wild root plants were first, since they are grown by a simple process that is easy to observe and to copy from nature. Manioc, a starchy South American root from which we get tapioca, may have been one of these.

It's likely that no group attempted to grow more than one plant at a time. Early men did not plan or think very far ahead. They planted where they could and gathered wild fruits when they found them. But they still relied mainly upon hunting for food. Yet men did reach the farming stage in many different parts of North America about the same time, from 7,000 B.C. to 5,000 B.C. Earliest farming probably began in the Valley of Mexico. It developed to a high stage only after a long period of testing and changing new methods and crops.

When the first Europeans arrived in the New World, they found that many different types of squash were being grown on farms in widely separated areas. This was also true of beans, which ranked second to corn as a native crop. The one we know best, the common bean, was evidently first planted on farms in Guatemala, Central America, where its wild ancestor still grows today. But the Peruvian Indians, who were genuine plant wizards, developed the ordinary bean plant into the present-day lima bean. More than seventy plants used by the Peruvian Indians for food, medicine, or textiles, have been identified either from seeds found in ancient burials or from Spanish records of the conquest of Peru.

How did these various plants spread to so many different parts of America? We already know what great travellers these early Indians were. They made their way from the Arctic to the southernmost tip of South America without map or compass. They had no other weapons than those made from stone, bone, antler, or wood. They were also great traders who

carried their new plants to other tribes. The plants eventually reached areas which were far distant from the place where they were first grown. And as they travelled, these plants changed still further, adapting to many different growing conditions such as climate, soil, and rainfall.

But corn was the greatest achievement of these earliest Indian farmers. The corn we know today – with all those shining golden kernels, beautifully spaced and protected within the green husk of the long, slender ear – was not always that way. It has changed drastically over hundreds of years.

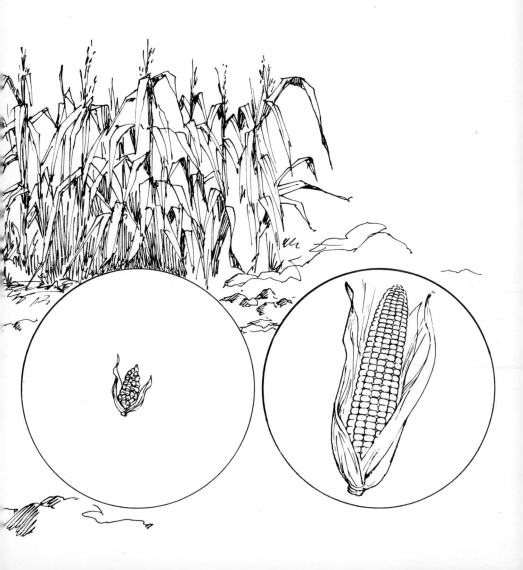

Originally the ear was much smaller and different in shape, looking something like a very large pine cone. Each of its kernels was completely enclosed in a tough, pointed husk or pod. This primitive wild corn, called pod corn, grew in the lowlands of eastern South America. In order to eat the kernels, the Indians had to remove the husk from each individual kernel – a long and tiresome process.

Corn became the tasty ear we know today because even these primitive Indians were thinking men. They probably already knew something about planting and harvesting crops, possibly root crops. It is believed that they noticed that the maize, which they gathered as a wild seed, sometimes produced a few kernels which were *not* enclosed in the tiny husks. By planting these kernels, they were able to grow ears of corn with fewer of the husk-enclosed kernels.

This process is known as selective planting, and it is practised by farmers today to produce better crops. The Indians did not know the scientific principles used today, but gradually, over many years, they produced corn with fewer and fewer of the tough husks.

Travellers carried this new corn southward into Peru. We know what it looked like because Peruvian pottery shows this small cone-shaped cob with its long pointed kernels. The pottery dates from about 2,000 B.C.

The corn also travelled northward into Central America. Here, further cross-breeding with another related plant, *trypsacum,* gave rise to new types. The ear gradually took on the shape it has today.

From these beginnings, the Indians developed many varieties of corn: the long slender straight-rowed flint corns, the pointed popcorns, and the dents, which have the gleaming tooth-shaped kernels we all recognize. And because these early Indians loved bright colours, they developed corn with kernels which were deep dark red, blue, speckled, black, white, yellow, and rich brown. We decorate with these at Hallowe'en, but the Indians included kernels of all these various colours in their sacred medicine bundles to ensure good crops. Even in modern times, the Zuni and Navajo Indians of the American south-west revere corn meal and corn pollen as "the source of our flesh."

Corn quite probably reached the south-west from Mexico. It was first grown in this high plateau region by the descendants of those first roving hunters, who arrived from Asia near the end of the last Ice Age. These early North American farmers are known as the Basket Makers and they lived in North America more than 3,000 years ago.

Until European explorers arrived in America, they knew nothing about maize, which is native to the New World only. And except for removing the gaudy colours, no real change has been made in corn, or in its cultivation, since that time. We still plant it in hills, just as the Indians did.

When men in North America learned to plant crops, they set their feet on the first upward rung leading to a more settled way of life. They no longer needed to be nomads, moving about in search of game. Planting crops gave them a more secure food supply. It made it possible for more people to live in one area and to develop community living. This more settled way of life eventually produced the civilizations of the Mayas in Mexico and Central America and the Incas in South America.

For all Indians, corn became the symbol of a more stable way of life. In their religious ceremonies, they continued to express their gratitude to the Great Spirit for this supreme gift of noble grain. This reverence and joy fills the Navajo song:

> My corn is arising,
> My corn is continually arising,
> In the middle of the field my corn is arising,
> White Corn Boy he is arising.

sticks three or four feet long, with the lower end broadened, in order to turn the soil; or sharpened to a point, these sticks were used to dig holes for seeds, or perhaps were used for weeding.

Eventually they tamed wild turkeys and made fine needles out of the turkey bones. They also dried the skin of these birds for cloth. They learned to grind the maize into meal – using almost the same type of grinding stone employed by even earlier men to grind roots, berries, and nuts. This grindstone, or *metate,* had a hollowed-out centre, where the corn kernels were placed. Then with the round handstone or *mano,* which fitted into the metate, the corn kernels were finely ground.

How do we know that these early Basket Makers were able to do all these things? When they learned to grow maize and to grind it, they found they could store it for future use when crops were bad. So they dug shallow storage pits two to four feet deep, usually separate from their houses. To keep the pits dry, they lined them with flat stones stood on edge. In such storage pits have been found not only remains of corn, beans, and squash, but also snares, nets, and weapons which the Basket Makers used for hunting.

These early people also used the storage pits as burial places. Skeletons found in the pits indicate that these earliest Basket Makers were a fine-boned, rather long-headed people. Their dead were placed in the pits and their heads covered with – guess what – baskets, of course.

These baskets always had black and white designs on the natural yucca fibre. Square-toed sandals were also found in the pits, as well as the skeletons of dogs. These had been buried with their masters, possibly as companions for hunting in the life beyond the grave. Even at that time the dog was man's companion and helper!

Over the centuries, other groups kept moving into the Basket Makers' area, and with new groups came new ideas

and improvements in the Basket Makers' way of living. Related families began to build their one-room houses closer together, until they all formed a single-storey structure of many rooms. Eventually, whole villages came to dwell in large, multi-storied buildings. Often they were built into a deep recess in the side of a cliff. Quite a number of these early cliff homes have been found in the Four Corners region of the south-west.

Such group cliff dwellings were easily defended against enemies. Usually they faced south and consequently were warm in winter. Tucked into the cliff, they were protected from rain and snow. Often they were located close to a spring, so the early cliff dwellers were assured of a water supply.

These early Basket Makers were the ancestors of the Pueblo Indians, who later built the great cliff palaces of Mesa Verde in south-western Colorado and the fabulous mesa-top cities in the Chaco Canyon of New Mexico. The Basket Makers' storage pits became great round subterranean *kivas,* religous centres for Pueblo men. These could only be entered through an opening in the roof. Inside, in the centre of the floor was a mystical hole, which symbolized the Pueblos' belief that their first ancestors had come long ago from the darkness beneath the earth.

But it was the Basket Makers who laid the foundation for the better way of life which the Pueblos achieved nearly a thousand years later. These earliest cliff dwellers were probably the first prehistoric hunters to give up their wandering life and settle down in one place. Their more settled, peaceful life made it possible for them to plant maize, to build better and more permanent homes, and to create other articles besides hunting tools. Eventually, their descendants learned to make real pottery and to weave fine cotton cloth. But all this really began with basket-making.

Chapter V

THE GHOST CITIES IN THE CLIFFS

Is it thrilling to read about explorers who find mysterious cities, abandoned and long forgotten, their walls in ruins, their palaces empty, with no trace of the people who once lived there? Four brothers, the Wetherill boys, who lived with their parents on a ranch in south-western Colorado, discovered North America's ghost cities. In 1890, Richard Wetherill, with his brother-in-law, Charlie Mason, set out to track down some stray cattle. They ran the cattle into a narrow canyon, where some of them got away again. Richard, trying to spot them, climbed to a high point where he could look down into the canyon.

As he glanced over the cliff on the opposite side, Richard saw, within a huge shadowed cave, the walls and towers of an enormous ruin, with a great round tower in the centre – a dream city! He could scarcely believe his eyes, but from then on, he kept a sharp lookout. That same day he saw another ruin tucked into a cliff. The next day, he found still another larger cliff city, with a square tower five stories high.

This time Richard and his brothers explored the ruin. This cliff palace, which was eventually called Mesa Verde, contained two hundred rooms. The boys crawled down into a deep round underground chamber through its only entrance, an opening in the roof. This was the *kiva,* the religious centre for the people who once lived in this cliff city in present-day New Mexico.

Word of the Wetherill boys' discovery spread and soon experts arrived to study the mysterious city. In its various rooms were found corn, beans, and squash, which indicated that the residents had been excellent farmers. There were tools made of stone and of deer bone, as well as fine needles made of turkey bones, and beautiful silver ornaments, inset with stones of cut turquoise. There were also scraps of hand-woven cotton cloth which once had been clothing.

These cliff dwellers evidently had tamed wild turkeys, for turkey pens and bones were also found, as well as blankets made of turkey feathers. It was plain that the people who had lived here had changed a great deal from the simple, primitive wandering hunters who arrived just after the last Ice Age.

Most wonderful of all were the houses which these Indians had built of stone, lumber, and masonry. Their cliff homes were really apartmenthouses, some of them four and five stories high. They were big enough to house many people, usually all members of related families.

Once these first cliff-cities were discovered, the search began in earnest. Many other ghost cities were found – not in the cliffs, but on the flat tops of high buttes and mesas. A mesa is a kind of high flat tableland, with steep sloping sides. Such sites offer a clear view in all directions, and are easily defended.

On the high mesas in Chaco Canyon of New Mexico are the ruins of at least twelve of these giant community houses. Some are rectangular, some oval, some shaped like a half-moon. Each of the upper stories of these vast apartment-like structures was set back so that the roof of the the next lower story formed a terrace, where families could work and sun themselves outdoors. Each dwelling had its door or opening in the roof, and could be entered only from the terrace below, by means of ladders. These could be pulled up to keep out intruders.

One such immense structure in Chaco Canyon became known as Pueblo Bonito. It rose five stories high, covered three acres, and contained eight hundred rooms. It probably housed

about 1200 people. The Spaniards called the Indians who built these mesa cities "Pueblos" – the Spanish word for "town."

The Pueblos planted their crops in the valleys below the high mesas. This south-west plateau region was dry, and these early farmers depended on heavy seasonal rainfall. To save rain, they built great dams and reservoirs to catch the heavy summer run-off. And they dug a network of ditches to carry the water from the reservoirs to their crops of corn, beans, and squash.

Life was good among these peaceful Pueblo people. Hard work and good behaviour were the rule. They were happy at work and at play. They sang to bring their corn up from the ground. They called rainfall down with puffs of smoke from their pipes. They cleaned up the town for arrival of the harvest, "so that the corn will be glad that we bring it in." The women ground the corn in a kind of community grinding-bee, while a man in the doorway played the grinding song on a flute. They cooked the ground maize into a delicious paper-thin corn bread on a hot stone or *metate.* These "tortillas" are made the same way in Mexico today.

The government of Pueblo towns was very democratic. In some of them, the summer people (those born in summer) took turns with the winter people in ruling. In other groups, the head of a certain society or clan became the town leader. Such men of authority were called elder brothers.

Why, with all these good things to live for, did the Pueblos desert their cliff homes and their high mesa-top towns? At the close of the thirteenth century, long before white men came to America, fierce nomadic tribes of Apachés and Navajos swept down from the north. They probably broke through the defences of the unwarlike Pueblo people, or perhaps they seized the farmlands in the valley and starved them out. It seems also that about this time a great drought struck this region, lasting for twenty-four years. The combination of these two disasters was just too much for the Pueblo people.

They abandoned their great terraced apartment-like structures, many of which had been added to for one hundred and fifty years. The Pueblos' golden age had ended. Their mesa-top cities stood empty.

The years passed. The Navajo Indians, who took over this area, knew of the deserted cliff-cities, but they were fearful of them. They thought that the spirits of the people who had lived there still haunted the empty dwellings. They called these early builders "Anasazi," which means "The Ancient Ones."

These remarkable cliff dwellers were North America's first great builders. They moved southward and eventually merged with other tribes. They continued to build villages and some multi-storied pueblos like Casa Grande, near present-day Phoenix, Arizona. But such structures never achieved the grandeur of the earlier ones.

Fortunately for us, we can see their great buildings in the ghost cities they left behind them. These are proof that these early Pueblo Indians, whose ancestors were the Basket Makers, reached the highest stage of development of any group of Indians north of Mexico.

Chapter VI

THE SHELLFISH EATERS

Man's earliest presence in North America is shown by such things as tools and weapons. Almost all of them have been found chiefly in the south-west region of the United States. If men lived farther north at that time, any stone tools they left behind were probably destroyed by the grinding power of the great ice sheets. Those glaciers advanced and retreated many times over thousands of years.

The first hunters were fleeing ice and snow and following game southward into the plains. Successive waves of nomadic tribes swept down from the Canadian plains over the centuries. The Apachés and Navajos who took over the territories of the Pueblo Indians were such people. Some Indians of this Athapascan language group still inhabit Canada's Northwest Territories today. But generally they did not settle in Canada until long after they did in south-western United States.

Not all of these wandering bands were hunters. Some of these early nomads settled along the Pacific coast and along the Gulf of Mexico. Their former village sites are marked by huge heaps of clam and mussel shells, which they left behind them. These shell heaps are found along the rivers and the coast from southern Alaska to the southern tip of South America. They appear so frequently that they may be some of man's earliest village sites. Such folk had few skills and got food in the easiest possible way. So they lived almost solely upon the plentiful shellfish. They are called the Shellfish Eaters.

Over the years the heaps of discarded clam and mussel shells grew higher and higher. The people built their primitive houses of small trees, covered with skins or thatching, right on top of the dumps. These vast heaps of kitchen waste, called middens, may not seem very impressive, but we must remember that shells are less perishable than anything else they may have used.

These settlements along both the Pacific and Atlantic Oceans may be some of the earliest attempts of primitive wandering folk to settle in one place. On the forested coasts of British Columbia, some of these early Shellfish Eaters became skillful seafaring fishermen. Possibly they were the ancestors of the Tlingits, Haidas, and other British Columbia coast tribes. These people never learned to farm because the great forests along the north-west coast made it impossible.

But along the eastern rivers and the Gulf of Mexico both climate and soil were ideal for farming. Across the Gulf of Mexico, in Central America, new ways of doing things were developing among an unusual group of Indians, whom we call the Mayas (pronounced My-ahs). They are famous for the grandeur and beauty of their great temple-topped pyramids, and for their bridges, aqueducts, and great stone ceremonial plazas. The Mayas attained the highest civilization known to ancient North America. Their influence spread through trading across the Gulf of Mexico. It reached the Indians living in the southern Mississippi Valley, and farther north up the river to the present State of Wisconsin.

The southern Shellfish Eaters learned to plant maize and to make pottery. Like the Mayas, they boiled their ground maize into a kind of corn soup. This method of preparing corn was quite different from that of the Pueblo Indians. Pueblos baked the ground corn on a hot stone in the form of a flat cake, or tortilla.

The southern Indians copied the Mayas by building huge, flat-topped mounds of earth, since they didn't have the stone which was available to the Mayas. On top of the mounds, which were usually located in a village square, were wooden temples. In such temples an eternal fire was kept alight. Usually it was renewed once a year in a special ceremony.

Farther west and north, just east of the Great Plains, other bands of Shellfish Eaters followed the river valleys which stretch from the Rockies to the Mississippi River. Such rivers are the Missouri, the Platte, the Arkansas and the Red River of the South, which today marks the boundary between Oklahoma and Texas.

Fluted missile points like those of the earlier Folsom Men have been found in a number of ancient sites east of the Great Plains. These people were still hunters and gatherers of wild plant food. But over the centuries they settled in the rich bottomlands of the rivers and became part-time farmers. Probably they got seed corn from Indians farther south through trade. Some of them also got pottery through trade even before they learned to plant maize, beans, and squash.

The Spanish adventurer Coronado found the Pawnee and Wichita Indians settled in villages along the Red River of

the South. They built villages of single-room, circular, earth-covered houses, or round straw-thatched ones. Often these communities were enclosed within heavy stockades to protect them from the more warlike, nomadic tribes.

Farther north and east, a similar early farming people, the Mandans, had settled in North Dakota. The Mandans had such light skins that they have been called White Indians.

Gradually, over long periods of time, wandering tribes spread into the woodlands east of the Mississippi. Along the Ohio River, a remarkable group of Woodland Indians reached a high stage of culture. It ranks with the achievement of the Pueblo Indians, who learned to build great mesa-top cities in the south-western United States. These Ohio Indians are known as the mysterious Mound Builders.

Chapter VII

THE MYSTERIOUS MOUND BUILDERS

When European settlers moved across the Appalachian Mountains and into the Ohio Valley during the late 1600's, they found great man-made flat-topped earthen mounds. Others were cone-shaped. Some of these mounds covered more than one hundred acres; at least one was one hundred feet high. Some had great systems of earth walls, enclosing areas many feet wide. Most astonishing of all, some mounds were built in the shape of various animals, birds, and reptiles. The famous Serpent Mount in southern Ohio uncoiled along the edge of a cliff, like a huge green snake 1,254 feet long.

The Indians, when questioned about the mounds, only shook their heads. They knew nothing of the use the mounds had been put to, and nothing of the earlier people who must have built them. Nor did these Indians have any legend or tradition which might have solved the mystery of the mounds.

Who then were these mysterious builders? How were they able to undertake such tremendous building projects, which must have involved thousands of labourers and many years of work? Certainly the Indians whom the settlers questioned couldn't have constructed the mounds. They were simple nomadic hunters, with very little knowledge of corn-planting.

Where had the Mound Builders come from? Where did they go? Experts explored a few of the thousands of mounds scattered all over this area east of the Mississippi, from the Gulf of Mexico to the Great Lakes. They weren't able to find answers to many of their questions. But they did discover a lot about these ancient Mound Builders, who constructed the earliest of the mounds about 2,000 years ago. Those first mounds were used as tombs, possibly over many generations, for members of certain families. Such mound-tombs were supported by timbers, over which the earth was heaped. Buried with these early long-headed people were their tools made of rough flint.

But the mound-tombs of a later date contained much better weapons and tools made of copper, such as knives, spear-points, harpoon heads, and fish-hooks. These later Mount Builders had learned to mine and work the copper from surface pits in the Great Lakes area. This was a remarkable achievement.

Other articles found in the mounds tell us that their builders had learned to plant crops, to live in villages, to make pottery, and to smoke tobacco. Beauifully carved pipes of pipestone, together with many different kinds of ornaments made of shell, copper, or shining mica, show the increasing skill of these early builders.

It took nearly a thousand years, but in that time the Mound Builders of southern Ohio achieved the most spectacular way of life of any group then living in North America. They were surpassed only by the Mayas, who were building their great stone temple-topped pyramids in Mexico and Central America at this time.

The most elaborate mounds were built by a group of Indians called the Hopewell Mound Builders of southern Ohio. Some experts have a curious theory about these people to account for their superior skills. They think that this particular group of Mound Builders moved into this area from still farther south. They may have brought with them new ideas, new fashions, and new skills from some much more highly developed region such as Central America.

No one can be certain about this, but we can be sure that these Hopewell Mound Builders were North America's first great traders. They traded raw material – pipestone, seashells, and metals – all over eastern and central North

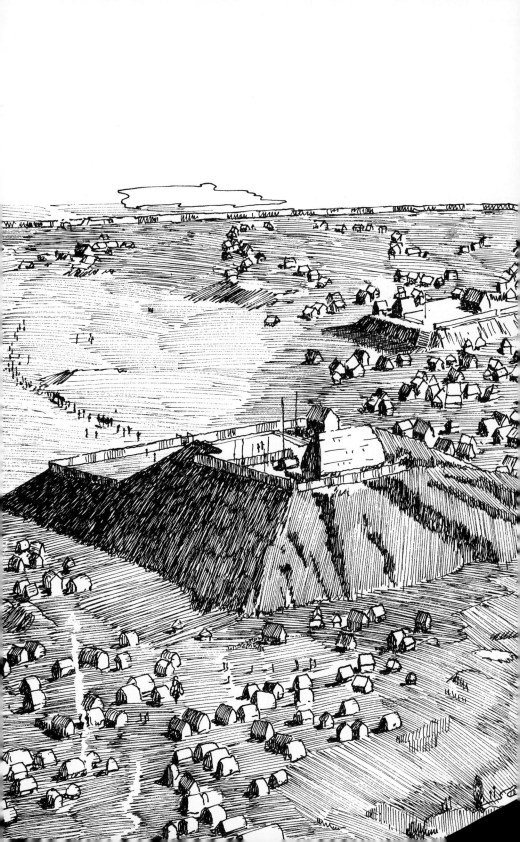

America, from the Rockies to the Atlantic. From Yellowstone Park in Wyoming they carried back obsidian, the hard volcanic glass which makes the hardest knife blades. From the Atlantic they brought sea shells. From the Gulf of Mexico they got sharks' teeth, and from the Rockies, grizzly bears' teeth. All these they used for ornaments.

In the great earthwork systems they build have been found objects made of gleaming mica from the Appalachian Mountains. Weapons, tools, and ornaments made of copper mined around the Great Lakes are also found there. The Mound Builders wore breastplates and helmets, beaten and hammered from copper, silver, and even meteoric iron. They loved fresh-water pearls which filled the lakes and rivers at this time. More than 60,000 pearls were found in one tomb. All this trade suggests they had well-organized trade routes, covering great distances.

The Hopewell Mound Builders were also skilled craftsmen. They cut mica into large sheets to line their immense burial places. They even made fake pearls from mica, by carefully coating it on tiny bits of wood. They wove mats and made beautiful pottery.

All this work was done by hand. What is most amazing about these Hopewell people was the great co-operation and organization which they must have achieved for such building projects. Did they use slave labour – perhaps captives from other conquered groups? No one knows.

Were their complex society and their wide-spread trading activities made possible by a loose union of tribes? Again, we do not know.

The objects found in the mounds tell us much about the Mound Builders' achievements. But we do not know with any certainty how they happened to reach this high stage of development. Nor do we know what became of them. It's like reading a book from which the front and back pages have been torn out.

We do know that in the period just before Europeans arrived in the New World, there was great unrest among the various Indian groups. There was a lot of moving about from one area to another; groups kept pushing into one anothers' territory. Buffalo were very plentiful on the plains, and in the eastern forests. Buffalo-hunting offered a freer and easier way of living than farming. Perhaps the thrill of buffalo-hunting lured the younger folk away from their settled existence, which had made possible the Mound Builders' superior way of life.

Did the Mound Builders leave this part of North America, or did they simply sink to the level of the hunter-nomads who surrounded them? We do not know. But by the year 1200 A.D. the Mound Builders and all they represented had disappeared.

Indians who later occupied this eastern Mississippi area didn't remember them at all. Strangest of all, the territory which the Hopewell Mound Builders had occupied was for many years before the arrival of European settlers a sort of No Man's Land, which no Indian group claimed for its own. Perhaps there was some kind of taboo based on a dim but powerful memory of the mysterious Mound Builders.

Chapter VIII

BABY FACES
IN THE
JUNGLE

In 1858, an Indian farmer was hacking a patch of virgin jungle near the present-day city of Vera Cruz on Mexico's Gulf Coast. He felt his machete bounce off something harder than wood. Digging deeper beneath the tough jungle growth, he realized that whatever was buried there was something very unusual. When the object was finally unearthed, it proved to be a gigantic stone head, six feet high and eighteen feet around. It weighed over ten tons, and its face was very round and fat, with thick curling lips.

Since that time other similar heads have been found in the same area, and these characteristically fat-lipped, flat-nosed stone heads have come to be known as Baby Faces. What do they represent? What race of people dragged such huge heavy blocks of stone through the swamps in order to carve these heads?

These Baby Faces were carved by a prehistoric people who are known to us today as the proto-Olmecs. Close to 3,000 years ago, in their swampy island town of La Venta, which no longer exists, these proto-Olmecs erected huge sacrificial altars and rows of basalt columns. All these objects, like the stone heads, lay hidden for thousands of years beneath the jungle growth. These prehistoric people also made figurines of oddly distorted people and bearded men, although beards are almost unknown among Indians.

These mysterious Olmecs provided the "mother culture," or original source, for all the very unusual civilizations which flowered in Middle America. This region includes southern Mexico, Guatamala, Honduras, and the Yucatan

Peninsula. But no one has been able to explain why these various civilizations began here in this hot, humid, tropical part of the New World.

Where had these proto-Olmecs come from? We do not know. But 4,000 years ago, before they arrived, other people were living in permanent villages in the Valley of Mexico and farther south in Guatamala. They were raising both corn and cotton, and in the course of the next thousand years they learned to make pottery and to carve small clay figurines.

Then, for unknown reasons, new ways of doing things appeared among these prehistoric Indians. It seems that new people, possibly proto-Olmecs, moved in. They brought with them a strange religion which included a snarling half-human jaguar head. In Mexico, these newcomers developed their most important centres, like La Venta, along the swampy Gulf coast.

To the south-east of these proto-Olmecs, of whom we know very little, another group of Indians were developing a civilization which soared far above the earlier Olmec culture. These were the Mayas, who also started as primitive corn-growing, pottery-making people. The Mayas were scattered in small tribes in Guatamala and Honduras, but all spoke the same language.

As the centuries passed, the Mayas perfected the loom and wove beautiful cotton cloth. They developed a system of picture-writing similar to that of the Chinese. No other Indians in the New World, not even the Incas in South America, had a written language as advanced as that of the Mayas.

Like many of the other races in this heartland of America, the Mayas built great flat-topped pyramids and crowned them with temples. But the Mayas were better than all these other prehistoric peoples in skillfully carving stone and wood, and in stucco-modelling and in painting the walls of their magnificent ceremonial centres. So superior was Mayan art that it became the source of later cultures.

For many hundreds of years, no one knew anything about the Mayas, for their empire, after centuries of civil war, had declined long before America was discovered. The Spaniards heard reports of the ruins of an ancient civilization hidden in the jungles. But they were looking for treasure, not ruins. So the great temple centres, built by the Mayas, became more and more deeply hidden by jungle growth. People even forgot the old rumour about lost cities.

Then two explorers, Frederick Catherwood, an English architect, and John Lloyd Stephens, a New York lawyer, de-

cided to see for themselves. In 1839, they found at Copan in Honduras the ruins of immense stone buildings, temples, and huge flat-topped pyramids, almost hidden by the enfolding jungle growth. Farther north in the Yucatan, the peninsula which juts out into the Gulf of Mexico, they found magnificent Chichen Itza, another temple centre. It had monumental stairways, ceremonial plazas, aqueducts, and bridges – all of cut stone. All these ruins, although so widely separated, were the products of a single culture. They had discovered the lost world of the Mayas.

But what did these ruins reveal about the people who built them? The observatories which the Mayas built on top of their great pyramids were used by priest-astronomers. These men worked out the movement of the moon and the dates of solar eclipses. To do all this, they had to be highly-skilled mathematicians. The Mayas were using the zero long before this symbol was thought of by anyone else. Stone codices were the ancient books or records which the Mayas kept. They show that the Mayas developed a more accurate calendar at least 1300 years before 1582, when Pope Gregory established the calendar which we use today.

But strangely enough, the priest-astronomers made little practical use of these important discoveries. They merely measured time to determine the dates of their religious ceremonies. As for the magnificent temples, palaces, and plazas, they were ceremonial centres only. The ordinary Mayas were simple maize farmers who lived in houses of pole or thatch. They trooped into these centres only to take part in religious pageants.

The Mayas weren't even good farmers. They were wasteful because they hacked down and burned trees and brush and planted cornfields in the rough clearings. When this land no longer produced good crops, they just moved on and slashed out a new clearing, using up the land. Although the Mayas build great aqueducts to supply water, they did not understand irrigation for their crops. Yet irrigation had been practised by the more primitive Pueblo folk, even before the time of the Mayas.

There were no minerals in the hot jungle lowlands of Middle America, so the Mayas made no metal tools. They used stone ones chiefly. Later on, they got objects of gold and silver through trade with Peru and Mexico. They had no household animals of any kind, except dogs. Strangest of all, they never developed the wheel for hauling, although toys they left behind them such as toy crocodiles are mounted on crude wheels.

The Mayas seem to have been very impractical. So many questions about them remain unanswered. Why did they abandon their magnificent ceremonial centres in Guatamala and Honduras and move farther north into the even more hot and humid regions of Yucatan? Had drought or pestilence struck, or crops failed? Or had the Mayas' wasteful methods of farming finally used up all the farm land? We do not know.

The Mayas tattooed their bodies and painted them in many different colours. They apparently never developed any organized political government. Priests ruled their daily lives and everything in Mayan life revolved around their holy calendar.

Today, the descendants of those ancient Mayas are a primitive folk, who hunt, fish, and plant a little corn. Nonetheless, they look as if they might have stepped from an ancient Mayan wall painting. The whole story of the Mayas is still a mystery. Their books and records were destroyed by the Spaniards. So the lost world of the Mayas is still largely lost to us.

Chapter IX

THE AZTECS

When Cortez's Spanish explorers first discovered the Aztecs' wonderful city of Tenochtitlán, it appeared before their astounded eyes like something out of an *Arabian Nights* tale. Here were the great towers and temples, rising out of the shining waters of Lake Texcoco. And great stone causeways eight paces wide joined the islands on which the city was built, on the present site of Mexico City.

Here was the vast columned central market place, with foodstuffs and fruits in abundance. Flowers were everywhere, for the Aztecs loved them, just as the Mexicans do today. To supply the city with fresh water, a three-mile-long aqueduct was built to carry the water from the mainland.

Mexico City's vast central square, or zocalo, in those earlier days enclosed a much greater area. In it there were twenty-five temple pyramids. These were built of earth and stone, but unlike the pyramids of Egypt, they had flat tops. On these flat tops were the altars and sacrificial stones. Here the priests of Huitzilopochtli, the Aztecs' dark god of war, slew hundreds of prisoners every day. The Aztecs believed that these human sacrifices were necessary to please their god.

People crowded the streets and squares, among them nobles and warriors with tall feathered head-dresses, carrying shields decorated with golden disks. Dignitaries were there, too, hung with jewels of gold, jade, and pearls. Farmers, stonemasons, featherworkers, silversmiths, and goldsmiths worked at their various crafts.

All this power and wealth the energetic Aztecs had acquired by constant conquests. Just three hundred years before, in the middle of the thirteenth century, they had been only one of numerous tribes of simple, warring nomads. These tribes had wandered down into Mexico from the north-west. Later the Aztecs, or Mexica, fled from enemies into the so-called "Valley" of Mexico, which actually lies at an altitude of nearly a mile and a half. Here, on a group of small, marshy islands, in the middle of Lake Texcoco, the Aztecs built their village of reed and mud shacks. It was to become their magnificent capital city, Tenochtitlán.

Over the centuries they grew in strength, until they had conquered most of Mexico. Their village on the islands was enlarged by reclaiming adjacent swampland. With forced labour from conquered tribes, they built great blocks of buildings. Wealth poured into Tenochtitlán, as payment from the conquered peoples. Not only foodstuffs, but gold, silver, jadeite, turquoise, pearls, and jewel-coloured feathers of the quetzal bird were given to them.

Little of their rich and elaborate way of life was their own. The Aztecs were still simple and violent people whose lives centred on fighting, conquering, and enslaving other tribes. But they were clever imitators. They absorbed not only the possessions and land of the more civilized peoples in Mexico. They also took over their culture and even their history, legends, and religion.

Who were these earlier people, whom the Aztecs first conquered, then imitated? Whenever you hear words with the hard sounds of *x, tz,* and *k* or hard *c,* you can be sure these are Mexican Indian words. These sounds are in the tribal names of such people as the Olmecs, Totonacs, Zapoteks and Mixtecs. All of these tribes built little towns and cities and flat-topped pyramids all over Mexico. About the same time, the early Mayas were building their great ceremonial centres in Honduras and Guatamala.

The Olmec culture reached its peak in the Valley of Mexico between 1200 and 400 B.C. It influenced the art, sculpture, and buildings of later cultures in Mexico. The Valley is actually a 3,000 square mile basin at altitudes from six to 9,000 feet, surrounded by mountains. It was the site of America's first farming society. And the earliest city centre was there, too. The magnificent Teotihuacán, which covered more than eight square miles, was that city. It numbered close to 60,000 people.

This first great Mexican Empire was overthrown by the conquering Toltecs, a group made up of many different tribes. The Toltecs rose to power around 1,000 A.D. They burned Teotihuacán about 600 A.D. All that is left today of this once great city are the massive temples, the pyramids of the Sun and the Moon. They can be seen today about thirty miles north-east of present-day Mexico City.

The Toltecs were probably Mexico's most notable people. They were conquerors and magnificent builders who built their own great capital city, Tula, north of Lake Texcoco. They also advanced the arts of peace. Metal-working was introduced into Mexico during this period. Trade increased enormously and luxury goods travelled to all parts of Middle America and farther north into the American south-west, where the Pueblo people had built their cliff-cities.

The Toltecs extended their empire as far as the Yucatan Peninsula, conquering the Mayans there. In its turn, the Toltec Empire fell in a furious civil war, and the great city of Tula was destroyed. Even its location was unknown for nearly eight hundred years.

All this took place long before the Aztecs arrived. However, the Toltecs definitely left their mark upon Mexico. Their religion, based on the Legend of Quetzalcoatl, whose symbol is the feathered serpent, was adopted by the Aztecs. The feathered serpent represented the source of all life to ancient Mexicans. The feathered wings of the "quetzal" (bird) was a symbol of the sky; "coatl" (serpent) was the symbol of the earth. Among the Mayas, this god was called Kulkulcan, which means "feathered serpent" in the Mayan language.

According to the legend, Quetzalcoatl was a priest-king who took the name of the god, as was the custom. To this priest-king, the Toltecs ascribed all that was good or intelligent in the world. He was said to have introduced both the weaving of cotton and the firing of pottery from clay. They believed that he invented the calendar and the art of picture-writing.

Quetzalcoatl was represented not as a dark Indian, but as a fair, and strangely enough, bearded man. The legend says that Quetzalcoatl went away to the east, but promised that someday he would return. The bearded white god would someday return from the sunrise to reclaim his kingdom. This proved to be part of the Aztecs' undoing, for it made them believe that the Spaniards were the returning gods. It was very easy for the Spanish to conquer them at first.

Also, the Aztecs' long and cruel reign over many other Mexican tribes caused their enemies to fight as allies of Cortez, the Spanish leader. The Aztecs' last ruler, Montezuma, also kept them from attacking the Spaniards at a time when they could have been completely destroyed. After Montezuma's death, the Aztecs rallied and drove Cortez and his small army of 1400 soldiers from Tenochtitlán. In this forced retreat, more than eight hundred Spaniards lost their lives. Some were killed in battle. Others drowned in the canal as they fled over the causeway, which the Indians had cut.

But Cortez, with many more troops, returned the following year. They besieged Tenochtitlán and starved out its people. The Aztecs fought from building to building, from street to street. More than 100,000 Aztecs died, out of a city of 300,000 people. That marked the end of the Aztec kingdom. A race of conquerors met the equally fierce Conquistadors and lost.

Ancient Teotihuacán, long-remembered by the Indians as "the place where the Gods reside," had been destroyed by the Toltecs. Tenochtitlán, the Aztecs' proud city, was leveled by the Spaniards. But on its ruins, Cortez began the construction of what is today one of North America's most beautiful al cities, Mexico City.

Chapter X

STATUS SEEKERS OF CANADA'S NORTH-WEST COAST

One of the most unusual and remarkable Indian cultures of all developed in Canada, on the north-west coast of British Columbia. It included the tribes we know as Tlingit, Haida, Kwakiutl, Tsimshian and Nootka. Farthest north were the Tlingit, who lived in the coastal reaches of southern Alaska. The Haidas lived in the Queen Charlotte Islands, just south of Alaska; the Tsimshian lived about midway down the coast. The Kwakiutl were farther south, and the Nootkas, who actually harpooned whales from huge dug-out canoes, lived on the west coast of Vancouver Island. They spoke many different languages, yet all these tribes had a great deal in common.

All of them were seafaring fishermen. In the summer they caught salmon, cod, and halibut. Their women collected roots and berries in the tall, lush coastal forests. They built their villages of gabled plank houses on the shores of the many inlets which knife into this 1200-mile coastline. Seal and other valuable fur-bearers, like the sea otter, were plentiful. The climate was mild, food was easy to get and life was comfortable.

These north-west-coast Indians were skillful craftsmen who created a wealth of decorated blankets, baskets, and elaborately carved chests. Collecting material goods was necessary to achieve status in their society. They placed great emphasis on the ownership of such property as blankets, sea otter furs, and "coppers," which were the shield-shaped plates they used as money. But above all, they valued slaves. They

was their way of getting supplies. But it turned into a giant, destrucyive give-away contest many years later when the white men came, bringing their endless supply of strange new goods.

Today, we would call such persons status seekers – people who emphasize wealth and social position above all. Ownership of property was the sign of both rank and social position with these north-west coast Indians. Often rank was inherited, for there were nobles among them. Membership in secret societies was also inherited. But wealth was a means of keeping or getting higher rank. It was almost an obsession with these Indians. They were genuine status seekers.

The ready supply of food and material goods allowed these people alot of free time to develop elaborate art. Their skillful basketry, blanket-making, and wood-carving were unsurpassed. But once again these Indians demonstrated their love for the fancy and showy. Every inch of space in their wood-carving was used for fantastic interlocked designs. Their boats and the fronts of their houses were heavily carved. Tall totem poles, carved and painted with the family crest, were monuments to the family's importance and the rank of its members. The design might tell the story of the clan's animal ancestor, and other related legends.

Methods and skills varied considerably along this long coastal strip. The northernmost tribes, Tlingit and Tsimshian, made the famous Chilcat blanket, woven by their women in black, yellow, and turquoise, from cedar bark and the hair of the wild mountain goat. Weaving this design had religious significance.

The Haidas of the Queen Charlotte Islands and the Kwakiutl were outstanding wood-carvers. Related families lived in large plank houses, with the house posts and door posts carved and painted with the family crest. Sculptors made carvings of wood, ivory, bone, and argillite, which is a one similar to slate.

All the advanced groups of Indians in other regions, like the Pueblos and the Mound Builders, owed much to Mexico and to races farther south, like the Mayas. But these north-west-coast Indians were cut off by the Rocky Mountains from any such contact. They developed their remarkable way of life without first learning to farm or to make pottery. Both of these skills have elsewhere been necessary steps in man's progress.

These north-west Indians never learned to plant crops, partly because the dense forests and steep hillsides made farming difficult, and partly because the sea supplied much of their food, including flesh and fish and even edible seaweed. Timber from the great cedar trees supplied material for their homes and for their great dug-out canoes. The timber was also used for the expertly made waterproof boxes which they used for cooking pots. Women wove the shredded cedar bark into blankets and cloth. They made the round, broad-brimmed basketry hats which they wore as protection against the heavy coastal rains.

These Indians looked different, too. Unlike most other North American Indians, they had mustaches and even beards. In their cone-shaped straw hats they looked much like Chinese. In warfare, the Tlingit wore wooden helmets with face covers and body armour of hardwood slats, similar to early Japanese armour.

All these characteristics seem to indicate that Asiatic influences were stronger here. We must remember that these Pacific Coast Indians were shut off by mountains and forests from the rest of North America. Original influences from north-east Asia, which lay just across the Bering Strait less than sixty miles from Alaska, were less likely to have changed over the centuries.

These Indians' strong sense of property and their emphasis upon social classes seem distinctly oriental. And the Chinese have a similar dread of "losing face," that is, of hav-

brothers. Many of the Indian clans, such as the Bear clan and the Buffalo, claimed descent from the spirits of these particular animals.

But hunting was not a very dependable source of food. Often there were lean times, especially among the Indians of Canada, who lived too far north to grow corn. Many of these northern Indians, like the Ojibwa and Cree, never changed from hunting to farming. They remained wandering hunters. When hunting was poor, famine struck and the starving people died. They believed that at these times the dark forest was invaded by unfriendly spirits, which disturbed the friendly woodland spirits. They whispered of Wendigo, "the monster of the north woods," who crept in among the bark lodges when Indians starved.

Hunting as a livelihood also required a great deal of land. Though each tribe had its own hunting area, there was a great deal of moving about. Trespassing by another tribe was often the cause of intertribal wars. They fought with arrows, war clubs, and tomahawks. They took prisoners and tortured them to test their courage, or slew them and collected the enemies' scalps as trophies of a warrior's skill.

Yet their warring was never on the large scale of the powerful and cruel Aztecs of Mexico. The Aztecs established complete rule over neighbouring tribes and demanded payment from them. These Woodland Indians of the north-east were raiders, not conquerors. In fact, ex-enemies often became allies. Defeated tribes were absorbed by the victors and adopted into the tribe, much as immigrants are treated today.

At times, some of these tribes achieved loose confederacies, or unions. In spite of sudden raids between forest tribes, there was a great deal more peace than war. Only under peaceful conditions could the widespread trading, which was typical of these eastern Woodland Indians, have been possible. Trade was carried on over long distances, along trade

routes over well-established trails. Lake Superior copper was traded to Florida; Minnesota pipestone went up the Ohio River valley to New York, and north into Canada; Virginia tobacco found its way to the St. Lawrence, and even obsidian from the Rockies was brought east to Ohio.

We do not know what these north-eastern Woodland people owed to the Mound Builders. The Mound Builders left no traces of their skills and arts among the forest people who followed them. However, almost all of the Woodland Indians valued seashells and used them as a kind of money. This custom may have begun with the Mound Builders. The seashells, which the Woodland Indians carried on strings, or braided into belts, were known as *wampum.* The Indians also exchanged wampum belts as ceremonial pledges of peace between the various tribes.

The names of all the tribes of Woodland folk who inhabited north-eastern North American are many and difficult. But they can be divided into four large language groups: Algonkian, Iroquoian, Siouan and Muskogean. To the Algonkian stock belong the Micmac Indians of Nova Scotia; the Chippewa, who lived north-west of Lake Superior; and the Crees, who roamed the unbroken woods of northern Ontario. The Montagnais tribes in northern Quebec and most of the Indians in the coastal plain of the eastern United States were also of Algonkian stock.

Between the Algonkian peoples of the Atlantic coast and those of the western Great Lakes were the Iroquoian people. They occupied most of New York State, as well as the region of the lower Great Lakes. Most famous of the Iroquoian groups were the Five Nations, five tribes whose land lay across the one good water route to the interior of North America. This was the St. Lawrence-Ottawa River trade route which led west to the Great Lakes.

The Five Nation Indians formed the famed League of the Iroquois, which continued for two hundred years. The tions numbered less than 20,000 people. However, the league did not always operate as a unit, except to obey its pledge against warring with one another.

They certainly warred with other Iroquoian groups. When the white men arrived, fur-trading became profitable for the Indians. There was fierce rivalry between the Huron Indians of Canada and the Five Nations for control of the western fur trade. It caused the Iroquois to destroy not only the Huron tribe but also the people of the Neutral Nation and the Tobacco Nation. All these tribes were of Iroquoian stock.

Everyone tends to associate the warlike Sioux with the Great Plains, but they were originally a Woodland tribe from the upper Mississippi Valley. They emigrated to the plains when they were driven out of their woodland villages by the Chippewa Indians, armed with French trade guns.

In the south-eastern woodlands, in western Georgia, eastern Tennessee, Alabama, and Mississippi, were the tribes of the Muskogean language group. These were the Choctaws, Chickasaws, Cherokees, and Creeks. All were members of the centuries-old Creek Confederacy, which was formed in 1540. They are sometimes know as the Five Civilized Tribes, because they so swiftly adapted to the white settlers' manner of living. Like the Five Nation Iroquois, many of these southern Indians became Christians. They were excellent farmers and stock-breeders. Many became wealthy, built beautiful homes, and even owned Negro slaves. They wanted schools for their children. They had written laws and a constitution patterned after that of the United States. They fought hard legally to retain their lands, but these Five Civilized Tribes fared the same as the others.

Once white settlement began to push beyond the Atlantic coastal strip, all these eastern Woodland tribes were forced to go to regions west of the Mississippi. Thousands died of exposure and disease on the way. For these once-free but now dispossessed Woodland Indians, their journey westward was well-named The Trail of Tears.

Chapter XII

THEN
THE
WHITE MEN
CAME

"This is the forest primeval.
The murmuring pines and hemlocks, . . . "

Longfellow

And the beech, and the ash, the birch, the elm, and the maple, the poet might have added. He was describing the untouched forest which everywhere met the eyes of the white men when they first arrived on the North American continent. The forest stretched from the rocky coasts of Newfoundland 2500 miles southward to Florida's palms and sand beaches.

To the white men, accustomed to cleared fields and busy cities, the forest appeared threatening. The trees seemed vast and countless. They reached to the distant skyline and far beyond. There were rivers, distant mountains, and a necklace of great lakes hidden in the unknown forest. Beyond the Alleghenies were still more forests full of deer and buffalo. In the shadowed depths gleamed a few campfires in the villages of the red men. To white men it was a trackless forest, but it was criscrossed by trails which only the Indians knew. These trails had been traced for centuries, as tribe traded with tribe. The rivers served as swift highways for their canoes. Still farther westward beyond the farthest rim of the forest stretched a sea of western grass.

Thus it had been for thousands of years. Then the Indians, peering from those eastern forests, saw the flash of white sails in the sun, like the wings of great birds upon the waters, where previously only gulls had wheeled and dipped. In fear and wonder, the red men welcomed the "People from Heaven."

This welcome was fortunate for the newcomers from Europe. They brought the thunder of their guns, their superior clothing, and their many technical skills. But still the godlike white men did not adjust well to this strange forested land. In the ghastly early years, these small bands of settlers could not have fought off the Indians, had they been unfriendly. Instead, the Indians showed the French had to counter the dreaded scurvy during that first long winter in Quebec in 1608.

The first English settlers in Virginia (1607) fell ill of deadly swamp fever. Chief Powhatan was the father of Pocahontas, the Indian princess who married John Rolph of the Virginia colony. He and other friendly chiefs sent corn to the starving settlers. Despite this help, only one hundred and fifty of the first nine hundred settlers survived that first year.

The Indians were equally friendly to the Pilgrim settlements in New England during their first year of near-starvation. The Indians showed the settlers how to clear the forest, how to set out their corn, and where to catch fish and game. New Englanders learned to like Indian cookery, from clambakes to baked beans and succotash (the green beans and corn which the Indians boiled together). The settlers learned to roast the wild turkeys, with which they celebrated their first Thanksgiving.

In Virginia, the Indians provided the newcomers with their first cash crop and first cash export – tobacco. The newly popular weed fathered Virginia's prosperity.

And how did the white men repay the Indians' kindness? They used the Indians while they were of use, in the early days of settlement. Then they pressed them remorselessly when they were less valuable than their land. There were some differences among European groups in their treatment of the Indians. But in general, all were chiefly interested in using them for profit.

The Spaniards had forced the Indians of Mexico and the American south-west to be Christians. They founded their first colony in that area in 1598. They presumably saved the Indians' souls, but at the same time enslaved their bodies. In Florida and in California, the Spanish gathered the Indians on missions and on farms as labourers. Later, when the great Spanish missions in Mexico and California were broken up, these lands became vast rancheros. The Indians were attached to the land as "peons," or slaves.

English settlers along the Atlantic seaboard were interested in trading with the Indians. The natives welcomed the white man's wonderful trade goods – guns, steel knives, woollen blankets, and whiskey. The Indians loved to trade. By the time Indian opposition to the white man developed, the settlers were too strongly settled to be chased away.

The English were the greatest threat, because they were primarily permanent settlers, rather than traders. They were ruthless in taking land. They found it easier to take the cleared fields of the Indians than to clear land for themselves. Indians were forced to sell and to move from their land for mere token payments. The Virginia settlers had very short memories. They forgot how the Indians had given corn to starving Virginia colonists. In later years, when the Indians experienced crop failures, the English settlers greedily traded their corn to the starving Indians for vast tracts of Indian land.

Only William Penn, the Quaker founder of the State of Pennsylvania, and Roger Williams in the Rhode Island colony, respected the Indians' rights. They paid a fair price for the land purchased or arranged for it by treaty.

On the whole, the French dealt more fairly with the Indians. In the beginning they were more interested in profitable fur-trading, rather than in getting land for settlement. They needed the Indians to get furs. Later they used the eastern Indians as middle-men in the fur trade with Indian tribes farther up the St. Lawrence, and those south-west of the Great Lakes.

Explorers like Champlain, La Salle, and Tonti of the Iron Hand sought new regions to expand the French fur trade. Devout French priests, intent on saving souls, accompanied the explorers into the wilderness. Champlain and Tonti reached the head of the Great Lakes and found a stream which led them to the Mississippi. La Salle continued down the Great River to its mouth. Their travels brought the French into conflict with the Spanish. The Spanish had founded a colony where the Mississippi flows into the Gulf of Mexico, in present-day Louisiana.

Meanwhile, English colonies had spread along the Atlantic seaboard, both northward and southward from Virginia. Settlers founded colonies in Maryland, the Carolinas, and Georgia. Here they came into conflict with the Spaniards in Florida. Later, English traders spread westward into western Georgia and Alabama. They were challenged by the French, who had established their first colony on the southern Mississippi River.

This conflict between French, Spanish, and English for land in North America destroyed the Indians. This struggle has been called the Anvil of North America – the Indians were caught between the hammer and the anvil. The Indians of the strong Creek Confederacy at first protected the English colonies closest to the Spanish in Florida. Much farther north, the powerful Iroquois Five Nation group defended the English against the French along the St. Lawrence, in the Great Lakes region, and in northern New York.

Both French and English forces employed the various Indian tribes as allies during the colonial wars which went on from 1689 to 1763. The wars ended with France's loss of all her territories in North America. Both nations "fought to the last Indian." Certainly many Indians were killed in these intertribal wars, which were part of the greater struggle for a New World empire. Many groups, like the Huron and Tobacco nations in Canada, were almost totally destroyed, or were broken up and moved into other areas.

But the white men brought the Indians even worse foes – diseases such as measles and smallpox, which wiped out entire tribes.

For a time after the defeat of the French in North America, Indian lands west of the Appalachians were secure. The English were interested in preserving the fur trade and they forbade settlement in the region west of the mountains. But the American Revolution brought about the end of British rule in North American colonies south of Canada. Settlers began to pour across the mountains. The Indians attempted in vain to defend their territories in this area, known as the Old North West. The flash of muskets replied. The white man's roads were cut through the forests, and towns sprang up alongside them. Fire and steel axes cut the forest away, thinning it westward.

Great Indian leaders tried to rally the tribes – Tecumseh, Little Turtle, and Black Hawk, the famous chief of the Sauks, who lived in present-day Wisconsin. For a while the Indians and the forests slowed down the rush of the settlers. But not for long.

Some of our history books picture the Indians as cruel savages, seeking to wipe out the white man's settlements with fire and tomahawk. Actually they were defending their right to the land which had been theirs for countless thousands of years. Despite their struggle, all the tribes east of the Mississippi eventually lost their territories to the newly-formed American states. The Indians were forced to move west of the Mississippi, in the so-called Indian Territory, which is present-day Oklahoma.

Manitou, the "tasselled corn-god," lost – not to the white man's God, but to the white man's greed. The white man's lust for land had replaced the right of the huntsmen, who had ranged over these forests since men first came to North America.

Chapter XIII

HORSEMEN OF THE GREAT PLAINS

When you picture Indians, do you always think of buffalo-chasing, wild-riding, recklessly fighting Indians? Do you think of proud, dignified chiefs, wearing stately war-bonnets, with feathers rippling down to their heels?

These are the Plains Indians as they are represented in North American folklore. They seem to embody all the wild, free, reckless spirit of the Great Plains. Yet very few of these "typical" Plains Indians were actually native to the plains.

Over the centuries, this area of long grass, just east of the Rockies, saw many wandering groups and invaders. Vast, open, and lonely, the plains stretched far as the eye could reach. They probably brought fear to those first early Stone Age hunters who came to North America more than 25,000 years ago. Yet the tall grass of the Great Plains was the haunt of many kinds of marvellous game. The wooly mammoth, the mastodon, and the Ice Age bison, with his hornspread of six feet, were there.

These prehistoric hunters probably also hunted the wild horses, which had evolved over millions of years. They were native to North America but died out here shortly before the close of the last Ice Age. By that time, the horse had migrated to the Old World, possibly by way of the prehistoric land-bridge, which once connected America and Asia.

Only a few of those early people actually settled on the Great Plains. The Spanish explorers came upon river-valley settlements of primitive, straw-thatched or circular earth-covered houses. The inhabitants cultivated beans, squash, sunflowers, and corn. However, other groups of nomadic hunting Indians preyed upon these village dwellers. Many abandoned their original settlements and moved farther east and downstream, where they built villages upon the bluffs and fortified them with moats and earthen walls.

The Apachés and Navajos were the earliest of these hunting raiders, coming into the plains from farther north around 1300 A.D. The Apachés attacked the Spanish settlements too and stole Spanish horses. Before they had horses these nomadic Plains Indians had used dogs to drag their "travois," which were A-shaped hauling frames made of trailing sticks. Though they hunted the buffalo, hunting parties stalked animals on foot, by creeping up on the herd dressed in the skins of wolves.

The horse, when it returned to North America with the Spaniards, completely changed the life of the hunters. Horses gave the Indians greater movement and speed. With galloping horses the buffalo could be surrounded, and if they stampeded, they could be chased down. The raiders, mounted

on horses, made life even tougher for the few settled farm groups. The tempo of the struggle increased and the area involved in this conflict widened. Almost all the farming villages collapsed under the impact of continuous raids. Most of them gave up the struggle and abandoned their villages. They, too, became nomadic Plains Indians, living in skin tipis, hunting the buffalo, and drying its meat to make pemmican.

The plains were certainly neither peaceful nor static even before the coming of the white men. They were always a kind of No Man's Land, for they offered a wide-open route for raiding Indians. The Kiowas and Comanchés, who were famed for their fierce attacks on wagon trains, swept into the plains out of the west and the north-west. Other marauders from the north were tribes of the widespread Blackfoot Indians, who occupied the Canadian plains.

Woodland Indians from east of the Mississippi, in their hunt for beaver, pressed first into the forest areas west of the Great Lakes. Eventually, many of them moved into the prai-

ries west of the Mississippi to hunt the buffalo. They, too, became thorough-going Plainsmen. The Woodland Crees from north-west of the Great Lakes in Canada became the Plains Crees. The famous Sioux, whom almost everyone thinks of as Plains Indians, originally lived in forest villages near the Upper Great Lakes in Minnesota. Moving westward, they became part-time farmers. However, by the late 1700's they had abandoned farming and moved into the Great Plains. Here they became buffalo-hunters and the wildest-riding warriors of the plains.

To the Plains Indians, horses became the symbol of a man's wealth. Horse-raiding among tribes became standard practice. Possessions increased in importance. With horses as pack-animals, huge tipis with thirty-foot lodge poles could be transported. Mounted Indians were able to slaughter the buffalo in great numbers after surrounding them with huge corrals. The trade in buffalo hides boomed. For a number of years, the Blackfoot delivered 20,000 hides annually to the traders at Fort Benton in Montana. The Indians did not realize that they were harming themselves by destroying game and encouraging white settlement.

This realization, when it came, came too late. The Plains Indians lived only for the day, and this period of prosperity was their greatest moment. Food was plentiful and easy to get. Consequently, they had more leisure – more time for ceremonies such as the famous Sun Dance, which was common to nearly all Plains tribes. There was also more time for practising fancy riding, fancy tricks, and fancy fighting. They also had more time for warring among themselves.

War had always been characteristic of the plains, but most battles were small-scale raids. Then, as the white man's frontier reached out to envelop the plains, the Indians' living and hunting space grew smaller. The buffalo herds shrank. The twilight of the Plains Indians had begun.

Chapter XIV

THE
END
OF THE
TRAIL

The American sculptor James Fraser designed a famous statue as a tribute to North America's Indians. The statue depicts an Indian warrior, weary and alone. Every line in his body and in that of his exhausted horse expresses utter dispair and defeat. That monument to the American Indian is known as The End of the Trail.

In the Great Plains lying between the Rockies and the Mississippi, the Indians of North America made their last desperate attempt to retain their freedom. Those wide free open regions were the last frontier for these nomadic hunting peoples.

The plains had always been an area of restless moving for many different Indian groups. But the Great Plains were actually the last part of North America to be invaded by the white men. Both California and Canada's north-west coast were known much earlier to European explorers, since these regions were easily reached by sea.

The Great Plains in both Canada and the United States were largely unknown and unexplored. A few French fur-traders had followed rivers westward to the Rockies over the American plains. They traded with the Mandan and Arikara Indians of North Dakota and the Pawness of Nebraska. In Canada, Hudson's Bay Company traders had established a trading post in the Saskatchewan plains.

France had lost its New World empire, but French *voyageurs* and Indians were still decidedly the muscles of the fur-trading companies in both the United States and Canada.

Indians served as guides for all the famous explorers. But these explorers and traders were not settlers, and the Plains Indians welcomed them. American free-traders, sometimes known as mountain men, were also moving into the plains and into the Rockies. They shared the wild nomadic life of the Indians, much as the early French *coureurs de bois* had done in Canada.

A great deal of warring went on between the various tribes who moved onto the plains. From the east had come forest tribes, the Sioux and Cheyennes, who had lived in the forested areas of Minnesota. Not only were they warlike, they were also expert with firearms. Both Cheyennes and Sioux became typical horse-riding Plainsmen. The Cheyenne soon came into conflict with the wild Utes of Utah and drove them deeper into the Rockies. The Sioux warred with the Crows, who hunted above the North Platte River. The southern Cheyenne battled the Comanchés and Kiowas, who had invaded the plains still earlier, around 1700. The Comanchés had already come face to face with the Apachés. Those much earlier raiders had harried the mesa-top cities of the Pueblos as well as the first Spanish settlements in New Mexico and Arizona. But the Apachés were no match for these newer and fiercer raiders. The Apachés withdrew to the western plains. They left the Kiowas and Comanchés, who were the plains' finest horsemen, in possession of lands as far south as Texas.

Meanwhile, Texas had been settled by Americans, although this territory belonged to Mexico. Later, when the Texans won their independence and joined the United States, more settlers flocked in. These newcomers believed that the primitive Indians were, in the frontiersman's language, "varmints" fit only to be killed. The settlers drove out many of the tribes, who had been driven out of their territories east of the Mississippi some years earlier. The supposedly worthless "Indian Territory," which the American government had granted to these Indians, had suddenly become very desirable.

In 1841, the first immigrant caravan crossed the Great Plains and arrived in California. The American settlers very shortly rebelled against Spanish-Mexican rule and set up an independent republic in 1848. That same year gold was discovered in California and the stampede for it started a tremendous overland rush to the west coast.

The Gold Rush raised California's population from 15,-000 to 93,000 within two years. California's Indians, who had numbered 100,000 in pre-Gold Rush days, were literally butchered. Only 30,000 were left in 1859. Eventually they were settled on reservations.

Then white settlement spread north from California to Oregon Country (Oregon, Washington, Idaho, and western Montana). The Indians here gave up about 85,000 square miles of their land at three cents per acre at the Great Council of Walla Walla. This treaty was opposed by many of the northwest tribes and they rebelled. Chief Joseph of the Nez Percé fought American troops for three years, but by 1858 Indian power in the north-west was broken.

The feverish search for gold continued. Around 1859, Americans, mining for gold in western New Mexico, aroused the Apachés. The Indians rose and almost swept Arizona clear of whites. This Apaché war lasted for ten years and cost 1,000 American lives. Eventually, the Apachés were subdued and settled on reservations.

More gold was discovered at the foot of the Rockies, near present-day Denver, in 1861. This Pike's Peak Gold Rush brought 80,000 whites into the plains within the next three years. Railroads were being built. The usual pressure for Indian lands began. Again and again, the American government broke its solemn promises, made in treaties, to protect the Indians' land. Buffalo hide hunters began to invade the plains in 1870. The buffalo, which was the Plains Indians' almost sole source of food, clothing, and tipis, became scarcer. Fighting again broke out.

To protect settlers and westward-treking caravans, American forts were built at important points in the Great Plains. Today movies show American troops battling with the Indians, but the white men did not always win. The Indians were led by such great fighting chiefs as Red Cloud and Roman Nose. Red Cloud held Fort Kearny in siege for two years.

The warlike Sioux had been guaranteed their lands in North Dakota by solemn treaty. Then gold was discovered there in the Black Hills in 1874, and another gold rush began. The Sioux fought desperately to retain their territories. In 1876, under Chief Sitting Bull and Crazy Horse, a Cheyenne chief, the Indians attacked. They battled General Custer's force of 250 men at the Battle of Little Big Horn in Montana and killed them all.

This victory marked the end for the Indians. Such an outcry arose against them that troops in great numbers were rushed into the plains. The Indians were attacked without mercy. Since they had no central source of supplies or warriors, their position was hopeless. They were separated into small bands and hunted down or driven into Canada. Sitting Bull brought his band into southern Saskatchewan. The Royal North-West Mounted Police eventually persuaded him to return with his warriors to the United States. Some remained and settled in Saskatchewan. The rest of the tribe eventually settled on reservations in the United States.

The Plains Indians' last stand was made at Wounded Knee Creek in South Dakota in 1890. Once again they were defeated and two hundred of them were slain, among them women and children. The sculpture called The End of the Trail shows a warrior, weary, defeated, and landless. It is a symbol of the fate of the Indians of the United States. By the end of the nineteenth century, all of them had lost everything to the white man.

Chapter XV

INDIANS OF CANADA – EAST OF THE GREAT LAKES

The explorer Champlain won the lasting hate of the Iroquois when he joined the Huron Indians in a raid into Iroquois country, south of the St. Lawrence near Lake Champlain. The Iroquois never forgave or forgot that defeat. The French in North America were threatened for nearly one hundred years with Iroquois attacks.

As a result, many people tend to think that the Huron Indians were different, perhaps more peaceful and less cruel than the Iroquois. Actually, there was little difference between them. Their people accepted torture as a way of testing courage and proving strength. Champlain, who wrote a shocking account of their methods of torture, also described public torture in Paris, the "centre of civilization."

The Hurons remained friendly to the French because they were the source of firearms, which gave the Hurons an advantage over their enemies. The Hurons also wanted the trade goods which the French exchanged for furs.

In those early years, the French supported the Indian world about them, for out of that world came valuable furs. Nor were Canadian Indians ever seriously threatened by French settlement in their hunting territories. Until the English conquest of Canada in 1763, French Canada's total population never numbered more than 60,000. These settlers were centred mostly along the lower St. Lawrence River.

Even when the English took over, the rate of settlement in Canada never compared either in speed or in numbers to that in the American colonies. Most Canadian territory lay much farther north than the American territory. It was less easily farmed and the climate was harsher. The forested areas, particularly those farther north, were difficult to clear. Rocks, rivers, lakes, and swamps made settlement difficult. Because of these difficulties, not because of better people, Canada's history is largely unmarked by the ruthless stealing of Indian land which took place in the United States.

Most of the Indians whom the first French explorers met in eastern Canada were nomadic Woodland tribes. They belonged to Canada's largest Indian language group, the Algonkian. They included the Micmacs, whom the French found in Nova Scotia around the Bay of Fundy (Acadia). These tribes also lived on Prince Edward Island, in the northern part of New Brunswick, and in part of the Gaspé Peninsula.

Along the St. Lawrence, Champlain met the Ottawa Indians. They were so-named not because they lived along the Ottawa River, but because they were noted intertribal traders. The word "ottawa" is simply an Algonkian term, meaning "to trade." The Ottawa River was this tribe's main trade route. Their tribal lands lay much farther west, around Georgian Bay in Ontario.

In northern Quebec, the Nascopi and the Montagnais Indians were also nomadic Algonkian hunters. The Montagnais tracked moose through the great woods north of the St. Lawrence. The Nascopi, farther west, followed the caribou onto the barren northern plateaus.

In Ontario, the Crees roamed the rugged northern forests of the province, while the Ojibwa, or Chippewa, hunted in areas north-west of lakes Huron and Superior. The Algonkian Indians, who gave their name to this whole language group, lived just north of Ontario's Iroquoian tribes, which included the Hurons and the tribes known as the Neutral and the Tobacco nations.

All these Iroquoian tribes lived much more settled lives than the nomadic Algonkian Indians. The Iroquois farmed as

well as hunted. They were able to raise enough food to last them through the long cold winters. Since they did not move from place to place in search of game, they tended to live in villages.

The European competition for furs created great rivalry between the Hurons, who traded with the French, and the Iroquois, who lived south of the St. Lawrence, mostly in northern New York State. The Iroquois got guns from Dutch traders on Manhatten Island in return for furs. To wipe out Huron competition for the western fur trade, the Iroquois literally wiped out the Hurons, the Tobacco Nation, and the Neutrals. It was in this murderous campaign against the Hurons that the Jesuit martyrs, Brébeuf and Laliment, lost their lives at Fort Ste. Marie, near Midland, Ontario.

There were no borders in those days to mark off Canada from what is today the United States. The Indians recognized no such rules in their wanderings. The Huron lands went unoccupied for many years, until Chippewa (Ojibwa) Indians came from their hunting grounds around Lake Superior and took over the region. Later, the Mississauga Ojibwa moved into the region of the Neutrals. Groups of these Mississauga Indians spread to many different parts of Ontario: to the Credit and Saugeen Rivers, to Rice Lake near Peterborough, Ontario, and to Kingston, Ganonoque, and the Bay of Quinte.

Because of their nomadic habits, many of the tribes who now occupy reserves in eastern Canada were immigrants to this part of North America. Today skilled "high steel" construction workers, the Caughnawaga Indians, live on the Caughnawaga Reserve near Montreal. They had come to Canada around 1650. Before that they had lived in New York. And the Abenakis, who today live along Quebec's St. Maurice River, came from the Allegheny Mountains of Pennsylvania when the French were defeated there.

Delaware Indians settled along the Thames River in Ontario after being driven from their homes in Ohio. Another group, the Munsee Indians of the Lenni Lenape, came from the United States in 1800 and settled at Muncey Town in Ontario. Much of this uprooting among the various tribes was due to intertribal warfare. But more often it resulted from the fact that the Indians took part in the wars between the French and English and later between the Americans and the English.

Following the American Revolution, Thayendanegea, better known as Joseph Brant, the famous Mohawk chief, brought many of his Five Nation Iroquois to Canada. His people wished to remain under British rule. The British government granted these Indians a valuable block of land. It included about 875,000 acres along the Grand River, near present-day Brantford, Ontario. Other Iroquois took up land near Picton.

But Canada was still being settled very slowly and land was plentiful. Canada's Indians first felt the threat to their means of livelihood – hunting – in the Maritimes. Here, shortly after Canada came permanently under British rule in 1764, a steady stream of farmers and fishermen emigrated from the New England colonies to the Maritimes. Later, following the American Revolution, many United Empire Loyalists flocked to New Brunswick, and the growth of farming and lumbering caused still more settlement on Indian lands.

Great Britain negotiated agreements and treaties with the various Indian tribes to pay for parts of their land. As early as 1765, such treaties were made with Indians in the Maritime provinces. Later, other treaties were negotiated in Upper and Lower Canada, when Scottish and Irish settlers began to arrive in considerable numbers.

The original money grants, yearly payments, and gifts which these treaties provided had at that time much greater value. They seem so little to us in terms of modern spending. Certainly they did not equal the value of the vast area of land they paid for.

Later, as still more settlers poured into Ontario and Quebec, laws were enacted to protect the Indians from aggression. They prevented settlers from taking away the reserves guaranteed to the Indians by the various treaties. More than half the land granted to the Six Nations on the Grand River had been lost to them before the government stepped in. The law still prevents sale of Indian tribal lands without Crown consent.

Indians were also helped to settle premanently on reserves which were suitable for farming. Yearly payments, which had been paid to individual Indians before, were used to buy houses, farming tools, and livestock. Today a great many of the northern Woodland Indians, like the Crees in Ontario and the Montagnais in Quebec, are still nomadic hunters and trappers.

Chapter XVI

INDIANS
OF
WESTERN CANADA

South of Calgary, on the Bow River in Alberta, there's a place where the swift-running waters of the Bow are shallow. This post, known as Blackfoot Crossing, had long been a favourite meeting place for Indians of the Blackfoot Confederacy. They were the largest and most important group of Indians living on Canada's western plains. In the fall of 1877, the Blackfoot, led by their great chief, Crowfoot, met with representatives of the Canadian government and signed a treaty. They surrendered all their tribal lands – about 50,000 square miles of territory in southern Alberta.

Never before had such a large group of Indians gathered at one spot on the Canadian plains. Besides the Blackfoot, the Blood, Peigan, Stony, and Sarcee tribes camped in the pleasant Bow valley. Tipis lined the river for miles, and the Indians' horses and ponies numbered more than 15,000.

Chief Crowfoot was outspoken for the rights of his people. But he realized that the day of the hard-riding, buffalo-hunting Plains Indians was nearly over. He was anxious for his people to live in peace with the white men. He realized that the Indians would have to adapt to a more settled way of life. On his advice, the Plains tribes traded their tribal lands for reserves. As a result, the Canadian West never experienced the bloodshed and strife which followed western settlement in the United States. Crowfoot's wise counselling won for him the title of "Father of His People."

Most of the Indian tribes west of the Great Lakes in Canada were of Algonkian language stock. East of the plains and in the northern forested areas of Saskatchewan and Manitoba lived the Wood Crees and the Chippewa, who were

hunters and trappers. French fur-traders were the first to meet these western Indians. When French rule ended in Canada, the great fur-trading Hudson's Bay Company was granted sole rights to all the lands in Canada west of the Great Lakes.

Neither this company, nor its rival, the North West Company, favoured settlement there. They realized that opening up these lands to settlers would seriously interfere with the fur trade. So the western Indians remained largely undisturbed in their hunting and trapping areas. However, the Cree Indians left their former forest land to hunt the vast herds of buffalo on the plains. These Indians became a thorough-going Plains tribe, known as the Plains Cree.

The great fur-trading companies delayed settlement of the Canadian West. But their efforts to extend the fur trade farther west were responsible for much of the exploration of western Canada. Henry Kelsey first saw the Saskatchewan

prairies. Anthony Henday travelled from York Factory on Hudson Bay and wintered with the Indians in Alberta. Both were Hudson's Bay Company employees. So was Alexander Mackenzie, who followed the Mackenzie River to its mouth in 1789. Simon Fraser also worked for the company. His dangerous journey down the Fraser River established Canada's claim to southern British Columbia.

These two Canadian fur-trading companies, which later joined, had excellent relations with the western tribes. They won the goodwill of the powerful Blackfoot Confederacy by their fair-dealing. As a result, the Blackfoot fought off American traders. They saved this part of the western plains for Canada.

The region which is today the Province of Manitoba was first opened to European settlers. It was easily reached by water routes from Hudson Bay. By this route Lord Selkirk brought his first group of Scottish settlers to the Red River district of Manitoba in 1812. He had purchased rights to a large tract of land in this area from the Hudson's Bay Company. But he also negotiated with Indian tribes of the Cree and Chippewa nations and he paid for their land. However, he had not allowed for the resentment of the North West Company. They resented this first intruder in their western fur-trading areas. As a result, the Selkirk settlers went through many hardships before the colony was finally firmly established.

It was not until after Confederation in 1867 that major settlement of the Canadian West got under way. The new government took steps to include the former Hudson's Bay Company's land within Canada's boundary. They opened up this entire area for settlement. American traders were pushing up from Montana, looking for furs and horses. They were tricking Canada's Plains Indians by trading cheap whiskey for valuable furs. The North-West Mounted Police force was organized in 1873 and sent west to maintain law and order on the plains. The western Indians learned to respect and trust the "Red Coats" as symbols of British fair play.

There was some unrest among the Plains Indians as settlers moved west. Occasionally, the Indians interfered with the surveyors and the construction crews of the Canadian Pacific Railway. In Manitoba there were Metis, who were part Indian and part white. They saw their livelihood as fur-traders threatened by the opening of the land to farmers. The Metis rebelled under Louis Riel in 1869. This revolt was put down without bloodshed and Louis Riel fled to the United States.

Between 1871 and 1877, the Indians of these western territories freely signed treaties giving up their land in Manitoba and Saskatchewan. The last of these treaties was signed at Blackfoot Crossing in Alberta. All the land from Lake Superior to the Rocky Mountains in Canada passed from Indian hands. In return, they received reserves. They were also given money to help them adjust to farming and stock-raising. The land given to the Blackfoot in the foothills of the Rockies was particularly good for cattle.

But in northern Saskatchewan it was difficult to settle the Indians on reserves. Chiefs Big Bear and Poundmaker and their tribes rebelled. More trouble arrived with the return of Louis Riel from the United States. Some tribes around Duck Lake and Batoche joined with the Metis in battle against the Mounties. Later a number of white settlers were killed at Frog Lake. Most of the western Indians refused to take part in the rebellion. Crowfoot would have nothing to do with it. It was swiftly put down by troops under General Middleton.

In Canada's Northwest Territories nomadic Indians of the Athapascan language group still live the life of wandering hunters and trappers. Members of this Athapascan group are the Slave, Dogrib, Beaver, and Chipewyan tribes. In general, Canadian Indians from east to west are adjusting to their more settled way of life. Canada's Indian population had dropped to about 100,000 early in this century. But it now stands at 265,000, about the same as it was when Europeans first arrived on this continent.

Chapter XVII

THE
ESKIMOS –
MEN
OF THE
ARCTIC

In the white frozen vastness of the Arctic, through long winters of almost endless nights, the green light of the *aurora borealis* provides the only natural light. The Eskimos, who call themselves Inuit, lived there as a separate race for thousands of years. They lived this almost completely isolated life until they made their first contacts with the early Norsemen around the year 1100 A.D. – long before the first voyage of Columbus.

The Norsemen called them "skraelingar," which means "little people." Compared to the Norsemen, they probably were small, for the Eskimos are definitely an Asiatic people: plump, heavy-faced, narrow-nosed, and long-headed. They, too, were immigrants from Asia. Compared to the Indians, they were late-comers. An earlier, very ancient Asiatic people is known to have lived in Alaska near Cape Denbigh perhaps as long as 8,000 years ago. These earliest Arctic people were very similar to those first hunters who came across the land-bridge connecting Asia and North America 25,000 years ago.

But the Eskimos were unlike the various Indian groups which came to this continent. They were Eskimo, not Indian, and they spoke a language which seems to be unrelated to any other language on earth. When they arrived in North America, probably not more than 2500 years ago, they were already well-adapted to Arctic living. They were Arctic hunters, skillful in using their *kayaks.* These were small one-man boats made of skins sewed over frames of driftwood. It is believed the Eskimos came in these boats across the narrow Bering Strait.

Moreover, the Eskimos chose to remain in the frozen northland. Nor did their way of life change to any extent over the centuries. They remained Stone Age men, for they hadn't learned to use metals. But they were certainly more advanced than those first newcomers to North America, who arrived on this continent toward the close of the last Ice Age.

The earliest Eskimos made small hand-drawn sleds, with runners of bone or ivory. It wasn't until much later that their descendents hitched dogs to larger sledges, or "komatiks." The newcomers also used ivory snow goggles with round holes. The goggles with slits were a later development. For getting about on the ice, they made a kind of ice-creeper. They lashed hob-nails of bone or ivory to their boot soles, much as the modern mountaineers do.

They wore well-fitted, carefully-sewed fur and skin garments, using fine needles of bone or ivory. Those early Eskimos had no pottery, but they did have the only lamps known to America. These were shallow saucers chipped from stone and filled with seal oil, with a floating wick of moss or grass. At first, these lamps were probably used only for light and a little heat. Temperatures often stayed for long periods at fifty or sixty degrees below zero. Later, they used the seal oil lamps for cooking.

They were hunters of Arctic sea mammals, such as the seal, walrus and whale. The earliest Eskimos settled along the Alaska coast in villages, where they lived in partly-underground houses of driftwood covered with sod. Some of the houses had paved stone floors and a central open hearth. Houses of Arctic peoples in Siberia today are similar to these. Eskimos in the western Arctic still build this type of house, sometimes with a long tunnel entrance.

Over thousands of years, groups of Eskimos drifted east from Alaska to Hudson Bay, Baffin Land, Labrador and Greenland. Although their language changed, today Eskimos in Siberia, Alaska, and Greenland can understand one another.

The Eskimo way of life was almost unchanging. Nonetheless, before the white men came to the Arctic with steel and firearms, the Eskimo people made tools far better than those of their ancestors.

They learned to make better arrows, harpoons, and spear-heads of whale bone and walrus tusk. At first, they had only hand drills with chipped stone points. Later, they developed the bow drill, a vastly better tool. Using the bow drill, they were able to shape soapstone, a native rock, into bowls for cooking. From soapstone they made the saucer-shaped stone lamps.

Eskimos in the central and eastern Arctic devised the famous vaulted snow house, or "igloo," built from blocks of snow. This type of dwelling was never used in Siberia. Canadian Eskimos trained dogs to pull their sleds. The dogs were hitched in tandem in the west, but fanwise in the east. They also made toboggans of baleen, a kind of whale bone.

For these Arctic hunters and fishermen, food was plentiful. In the winter, they hunted the seal with harpoons at breathing holes in the ice. And in the summer, they harpooned them with light kayaks, into which the hunter was lashed. At this time, they lived in skin tents along the seashore. A few of them went out in their larger, open boats, or "umiaks," to hunt whales with harpoons. The head of the harpoon could come off. When thrown, it lodged in the whale.

The Eskimos also made special weapons, darts, and snares for hunting birds. They built low dams of boulders across rivers, and speared the salmon trout as they travelled upstream. In the late summer and early fall, many of Canada's eastern Eskimos moved south into the Barren Lands, or tundra. On this great northern plain they hunted the caribou,

which provided skins for clothing and for tents. The herds also provided sinew cord, which the Eskimos wound tightly about their wooden bows to strengthen them. During the summer, Eskimo women collected roots, berries, birds' eggs, and shellfish for food.

Most of us have seen the beautiful soapstone carvings made by modern Eskimos. The earliest Eskimos, the ones who lived in northern Alaska, carved very beautiful work in bone and ivory, covered with geometric designs.

Canadian Eskimos' first regular contacts with Europeans were with whalers. They arrived in the Arctic early in the nineteenth century. The whalers introduced them to the use of wooden whaleboats, firearms, foreign foods, and steel tools. But the Eskimos' way of life changed very little. They continued to live by hunting and fishing. They moved from place to place, following the game which they needed for food and clothing. Basically they remained a Stone Age people, with special highly-developed skills.

The Eskimos managed to cope successfully with the harsh Arctic environment in which they chose to live. All too frequently the white men, equipped with all the special tools and weapons they have devised, have perished in the Arctic because they couldn't adapt themselves to the cruel hardship and cold. Even today, the inexperienced Arctic traveller needs the Eskimo to guide him from place to place, and to show him how to travel safely and how to protect himself.

Wandering Hunters
Cave Men (Folsom Men)

Wandering Hunters

Shellfish Eaters

Food Gatherers

First Farmers

Basket Makers

Olmecs

Mayas

Toltecs

Aztecs

Mound Builders

Cliff Dwellers

Pueblos

Pueblos

Eastern Woodland Indians

North-west Coast Indians

Plains Indians

Eskimos

10000 B.C.

5000 B.C.

1000 B.C.

500 B.C.

500 A.D.

1000 A.D.

1500 A.D.

1900 A.D.

FURTHER READING

For a more complete list of books for young people about the first North Americans, see *About Indians: A Listing of Books,* published by the Department of Indian Affairs and Northern Development and available through Information Canada, Ottawa.

Baity, Elizabeth C. *Americans Before Columbus.* Viking Press, New York, 1961.

Baldwin, Gordon C. *How Indians Really Lived.* G.P. Putnam's Sons, New York, 1967.

Bjorklund, Karna L. *The Indians of Northeastern America.* Dodd, Mead and Co., New York, 1969.

Bleeker, Sonia. *The Aztec.* William Morrow and Co., New York, 1963. The following Sonia Bleeker books are also available from Morrow: *The Eskimo, Indians of the Longhouse, The Sea Hunters, The Apache Indians, The Cherokee, The Chippewa, The Crow, The Delaware, Horesemen of the Western Plateaus, The Navaho, Mission Indians, Pueblo Indians.*

Brandon, William, adapted by Anne Terry White. *The American Indian.* Random House, New York, 1963.

Caswell, Helen. *Shadows from the Singing House; Eskimo Folk Tales.* M.G. Hurtig Ltd., Edmonton, 1968.

Clark, Ella. *Indian Legends of Canada.* McClelland and Stewart Ltd., Toronto, 1960.

Colby, C.B. *Cliff Dwellings; Ancient Ruins of America's Past.* Coward-McCann, Inc., New York, 1965.

Farb, Peter. *Man's Rise to Civilization as Shown by the Indians of North America from Primitive Times.* E.P. Dutton & Co., New York, 1968.

Jenness, Diamond. *The Indians of Canada.* McGraw Hill-Ryerson Publishing Co. Ltd., Toronto, 1966.

Kidd, Kenneth E. *Canadians of Long Ago.* Longmans Canada Ltd., Toronto, 1951.

La Farge, Oliver. *The American Indian.* Golden Press, Racine, Wis., 1960.

Leechman, Doulas. *Native Tribes of Canada.* Gage Publishing Co., Toronto, 1967.

McNeer, Mary. *The American Indian Story.* Ariel Books, New York, 1963.

Marriott, Alice. *Indians of the Four Corners.* Thomas Y. Crowell Company, New York, 1952.

May, Charles. *The Early Indians.* Thomas Nelson and Sons, New York and Camden, 1971.

Patterson, Palmer and Nancy-Lou. *The Changing People; A History of Canadian Indians.* Collier-Macmillan, Toronto, 1971.

Power, Ann Hervey. *Eskimos of Canada.* Collier-Macmillan, Toronto, 1971.

Powers, William K. *Indians of the Northern Plains.* G.P. Putnam's Sons, New York, 1969. Also: *Indians of the Southern Plains.*

Quimby, George I. *Indian Life in the Upper Great Lakes.* University of Chicago Press, Chicago, 1960.

Scheele, William E. *The Mound Builders.* World Publishing Co., Cleveland and New York, 1960.

Tait, George E. *The Eagle and the Snake.* McGraw Hill-Ryerson, Toronto, 1968.

Tunis, Edwin. *Indians.* World Publishing Company, Cleveland and New York, 1959.

Von Hagan, Victor W. *Maya; The land of the Turkey and the Deer.* World Publishing Company, Cleveland and New York, 1960.